Quantum Computers.
Are they our Future?

Nate Jenner

Copyright©2018 Nate Jenner
All Rights Reserved

Copyright © 2018 by Nate Jenner

All rights reserved. No part of this publication may be reproduced, distributed, or transmitted in any form or by any means, including photocopying, recording, or other electronic or mechanical methods, without the prior written permission of the author, except in the case of brief quotations embodied in critical reviews and certain other noncommercial uses permitted by copyright law.

Table of Contents

Introduction	5
Chapter 1- What is a Quantum Computer?	6
Chapter 2- How Quantum Computers Work	11
Chapter 3- Why do we need Quantum Computers?	21
Chapter 4- Will they Replace Classical Computers?	30
Chapter 5- Areas to be Revolutionized by Quantum Computers	37
Conclusion	46

Disclaimer

While all attempts have been made to verify the information provided in this book, the author does assume any responsibility for errors, omissions, or contrary interpretations of the subject matter contained within. The information provided in this book is for educational and entertainment purposes only. The reader is responsible for his or her own actions and the author does not accept any responsibilities for any liabilities or damages, real or perceived, resulting from the use of this information.

The trademarks that are used are without any consent, and the publication of the trademark is without permission or backing by the trademark owner. All trademarks and brands within this book are for clarifying purposes only and are the owned by the owners themselves, not affiliated with this document.

Introduction

Classical computers have not been able to perform certain tasks. This is due to their limitation in terms of computing power. Quantum computers can help in solving complex tasks that classical computers have not been able to solve. Classical computers also consume a lot of energy, and it has been predicted that we may lack energy to power computers in the near future. Quantum computers are known to consume a less amount of power, hence they will help in reducing power consumption. This book helps you understand everything about quantum computers. Enjoy reading!

Chapter 1- What is a Quantum Computer?

Quantum computing has grabbed the headlines. The word "quantum" itself is enough to trend, and after combining it with the computational power that has been so far it becomes irresistible.

An ordinary computer works based on 0s and 1s. Despite the kind of task you need a computer to perform, the underlying process is the same. The input, which is the task, must be converted into a series of 0s and 1s. The output is also generated in the form of 0s and 1s and the result is encoded. The processing is normally done by an algorithm. Regardless of how clever the algorithm might seem to be, all what it does is manipulation of strings of bits, in which each bit is either a 0 or a 1. In machines, this is represented in the form of electrical circuits, in which each electrical circuit can be open or closed. If the electrical circuit is closed, current will flow but if it is open, current will not flow.

Quantum computing relies on the fact that in microscopic world; things do not have to be as clear-cut as expected from microscopic experience. Tiny particles like photons and electrons can simultaneously take states that are seen as mutually exclusive.

The particles may be in various places at once, and photons are capable of simultaneously exhibiting two types of polarization. This type of superposition of different states is not seen in life since because it normally disappears once the system has been observed. Suppose you have a cat in a box. The cat can be either alive or dead as long as you have not looked at the cat. This is the idea behind superposition.

After measuring polarization of a photon or location of an electron, all except one of possible alternatives will be eliminated and you will only be able to see one. Superposition makes us free of binary constraints. The quantum computer normally works with particles that can be in a superposition. Instead of representing bits, the particles represent *qubits*, which take the value of either 0 or 1, or both at the same time.

You can oppose that superposition can be achieved using ordinary classical physics only, mostly by processing two bits simultaneously or something similar. In such a case, quantum computing will not be more amazing compared to classical computing. However, quantum computing has a lot other than superposition alone.

After looking at a system with more than one qubit, you will notice that the individual components are not independent of one another. The components can be *entangled*.

Classical Vs. Quantum Computer

The memory of a classical computer is made up of bits, in which every bit is either a 0 or a 1. A quantum computer is different as it maintains a sequence of qubits. Every single qubit may be a representation of a 0, a 1 0 even a quantum superposition of the two qubit states. A qubit pair may be in any qubit superposition of 4 states while 3 qubits in any superposition of 8 states. This gives us a formula that for a quantum computer of n qubits, it can be in arbitrary superposition of 2^n different states simultaneously. This is different from what we have in a normal computer as it can be in only one of 2^n states at any particular time. For a quantum computer to operate on its qubits it uses measurement and quantum gates and these are capable of altering the observed state. An algorithm is composed of continuous quantum logic gates and encoding of the problem is achieved through initializing the start values of qubits, which is the same to how the classical computers work.

In regular circumstances, the calculation ends with a measurement, and the system of qubits is collapsed into one of 2^n pure states, in which every qubit is either 0 or 1, finally decomposing into some classical state.

Where can you get a Quantum Computer?

Theoretically, researchers have seen a lot of potential in quantum computers, and scientists are working round the clock to discover this potential, a lot has to be done before quantum computers hit the market.

What is needed to build one?

To build a quantum computer, we only need qubits that behave in the way that we need them to. The photons may be made up of atoms, photons, molecules, electrons or something else. Scientists are researching these as they form the base for quantum computers. However, it is tricky to manipulate qubits since a disturbance will cause them to fall out of their quantum state (decoherence). The quantum error field studies how to combat decoherence as well as other errors. Researchers are everyday discovering new ways on how to make the qubits cooperate.

When will we have a Real Quantum Computer?

Quantum computers are already available, but they are not of sufficient power to replace the classical computer. Practical quantum technologies are emerging, examples being highly effective actuators, sensors and some other devices. Despite this, a true quantum computer that outperforms the classical computer is expected to be developed years in the future. Theorists are discovering new ways of overcoming decoherence, while experimentalists are coming up with new techniques and instruments of controlling the quantum world.

Chapter 2- How Quantum Computers Work

Computer manufacturers have generated massive amount of computing power. However, they have not been able to quench the thirst for speed and computing capacity. Our technological needs are growing each day, and a lot of computing power will be needed to satisfy these needs. Scientific research has generated a lot of data. Also, the emergence of the internet and proliferation of the personal computer has led to the need for more and more computing power.

The question is, will we get the amount of computing power that we need? According to Moore's Law, the number of transistors keeps on a microprocessor doubles after every 18 months, and it is predicted in 2020 2030, we will find circuits on a microprocessor that are measured on an atomic scale. Next, quantum computers capable of harnessing the power of atoms and moolecules to be used in processing and memory tasks will be created. Quantum computers are capable of performing particular calculations faster compared to any silicon-based computer. Scientists have built some basic quantum computers capable of performing some calculations, but no practical quantum computer has been developed so far.

Computers have been there for majority of the 20th century. Quantum computing was theorized for the first time less than 30 years ago at Argonne National Library by a physicist. Paul Benioff is known to be the first person to apply the concept of quantum theory to computers in the year 1981. He created a theory on how to create a quantum Turing machine. Majority of the computers that are in use today are based on the quantum Turing machine. If you are using a computer to read this book, it is based on quantum Turing machine.

Understanding a Turing Machine

A Turing machine is a theoretical device made up of a tape of unlimited length that has been divided into little squares. Each square can hold a symbol of 0 or 1, or it can be left blank. A read-write device then reads these symbols and blanks and these are responsible for giving the machine instructions on the action to perform. When it comes to a quantum Turing machine, the difference comes in that the tape exists in a quantum state as the read-write head. The symbols on the tape can be either a 0 or 1 or a superposition of 0 and 1. A regular Turing machine is only capable of performing a single calculation at a time, but a quantum Turing machine is capable of performing many calculations at once.

The computers of today, just like the Turing machine, work by manipulating the bits existing in one of the two states, 0 or 1. The quantum computers are not limited to two states, but they are capable of encoding information in the form of quantum bits, or qubits which can be in a superposition.

The qubits represents ions, atoms, electrons or photons as well as their respective control devices that work together to act like a processor or a computer memory. Because of the ability of a quantum computer to exist in multiple states simultaneously, there is a potential for it to be millions of times more powerful than the powerful supercomputers of today.

The superposition of qubits in quantum computers gives the *parallelism*. The parallelism in turn enables the computer to work on millions of computations at once, while your desktop computer is only capable of working on one. The computing power of a 30-qubit quantum computer will be equal to that of a conventional computer that is capable of running at 10 teraflops. The speeds of modern desktop computers are measured in units known as *gigaflops*.

Quantum computers have also taken advantage of another property of quantum mechanisms known as *entanglement*. Quantum computers have a problem in that after looking at the sub-atomic particles, you can bump them then change their value. After looking at a qubit at a superposition in order to get its value, it will assume a value of either 0 or 1, but not both. For a practical quantum computer to be made, the scientists should come up with ways of taking the measurements indirectly in a bid to preserve the integrity of the system. With entanglement, we can get an answer to this. In quantum physics, after the application of an outside force to two atoms, the two are entangled and the second atom embraces the properties of first atom. If it is left alone, the atom will spin in all directions. If it is disturbed, it will choose one spin, or just one value, while the second entangle atom will select the opposite spin or value. This way, scientists are able to tell the value of the qubits without having to look at them.

Qubit Control

Computer scientists use control devices for the purpose of controlling microscopic particles that act like qubits in the quantum computers.

These include the following:

1. Ion traps- these use magnetic or optical fields, or they combine both for trapping ions.

2. Optical traps- these make use of light waves for trapping and controlling particles.

3. Quantum dots- these are made up of a semiconductor material and they are used for containing and manipulating electrons.

4. Semiconductor impurities- these contain electrons by use of "unwanted" atoms that are found in semiconductor materials.

5. Superconducting circuits- this allows electrons to flow facing almost no resistance at low temperatures.

The Quantum Computers of Today

Quantum computers may replace silicon chips in the future, in the same way that the transistor replaced the vacuum tube. However, at this point, the technology that is necessary for us to develop a quantum computer is not available. Most of the research done in quantum computing is still theoretical.

The advanced quantum computers are not capable of manipulating more than 16 qubits, making them lag much behind a practical application. However, it is predicted that quantum computers will one day perform calculations that are time-consuming to the conventional computers quickly and easily. A lot of advancements have been made in the field of quantum computing. Here are some of the quantum computers that have been developed:

1998

MIT Researchers and Los Alamos spread a single qubit across three nuclear pins in every molecule of liquid solution of alanine (which is an amino acid for analyzing the quantum state decay) or trichloroethylene (which is a chlorinated hydrocarbon that is used in quantum error correction) molecules. After spreading out the qubit, it become a bit harder to corrupt, and researchers were allowed to use entanglement in order to study the interactions between the states as an indirect method of analyzing the quantum information.

2000

In March, the Los Alamos National Laboratory scientists announced that they have developed a 7-qubit quantum computer within a single liquid drop.

The quantum computer makes use of a nuclear magnetic resonance (NMR) to manipulate the particles in atomic nuclei of molecules of the trans-crotonic acid, which is a simple fluid made up of molecules of four carbon and six hydrogen molecules. NRM is used for application of electromagnetic pulses which normally forces particles to line up. When the particles are in positions that are counter or parallel to the magnetic field, the quantum computer is made to mimic the behavior of digital computers in which they encode the information in bits.

In August, researchers from IBM-Almaden Research center made what was termed to be the most advanced quantum computer. It was a 5-qubit quantum computer designed to allow a nuclei of 5 fluorine atoms do interact with the rest in as qubits, be programmable by radio frequency pulses and be detectable by NMR instruments similar to the ones used in hospitals. After this, they were in a position to solve a mathematical problem that a conventional would repeat many cycles in order to solve. The problem, which was known as *order-findind* involved looking for the period of a function, which is a typical aspect of cryptography mathematical problems.

2001

Scientists from Stanford University and IBM were able to demonstrate the Shor's Algorithm using a quantum computer. This is an algorithm that involves looking for the prime factors of a number. The algorithm is very useful in cryptography. A 7-qubit quantum computer was used for the purpose of finding the factors of 15. The computer was able to find that the prime factors of 15 are 3 and 5.

2005

The University of Innsbruck announced that the first qubyte had been created by scientists using ion traps. The qubyte was made up of a series of 8 qubits.

2006

Scientists in Massachusetts and Waterloo came up with methods for quantum control on 12-qubit system. This shows that systems had begun to use more qubits, making quantum control very complex.

2007

A startup company in Canada named D-Wave developed a 16-qubit quantum computer.

The computer successfully solved a Sudoku and some other pattern matching problems. The company has stated that they hope to create practical systems in the near future.

If it is possible to create functional quantum computers, they will be very useful in factoring large numbers and therefore very applicable in encoding and decoding secret information. If a functional quantum computer was built today, then there would be no safe/secure information on the internet. This is because a quantum computer is so powerful such that it can decode the encoded information within milliseconds, even the ones in which complex algorithms were used for encoding the information. The encryption methods that are used today are too simple when compared to what a quantum computer is capable of doing. When it comes to searching for data in large database, a quantum computer can do it in just the fraction of time that it takes a conventional computer to do the same. Quantum computers may also be applicable in designing other quantum computers as well as in quantum mechanics.

However, quantum computing is still in its initial stages, and computer scientists have argued that currently there is no technology that can help in the development of quantum computers.

Quantum computers should have dozens of qubits so that they can be in a position to solve the real-world problems, and be able to provide a viable computing method.

Chapter 3- Why do we need Quantum Computers?

In the today's world, we rely on computers to store and share information. Computers have made tasks easy; hence people cannot live without computers.

New trends have emerged since the discovery of the first computer. A research done by Semiconductor Industry Association has shown that if we continue with this trend, if the computing trends continue in the same way, by 2040, we will not be able to power all machines around the world. This is why the industry is looking for ways to make computing more energy efficient. However, with classical computers, there is a minimum amount of energy that they need in order to be able to perform tasks.

In 1961, it was discovered that in every computer, every single bit operation uses an absolute minimum amount of energy. A research was done to find the minimum amount of energy that is needed for a computer to operate, and it was found that it is possible for one to make a chip that can operate on that amount of energy.

This is capable of cutting the amount of energy used by computers by a factor of a million.

However, it may take some time before this technology is implemented on our laptops. This explains why computer scientists are looking for ways to turn into other forms of computing such as quantum computing.

Quantum computing relies on the ability of subatomic particles to be able to exist in more than one state at any particular time. Due to the behavior of tiniest particles, it is possible to do operations much quickly while using less energy than the one used by classical computers.

In classical computing, a bit refers to a piece of information that is capable of existing in two states, that is, 1 and 0. Quantum computing relies on quantum bits, which are quantum systems with two states. However, they are capable of storing more information compared to just a 0 or a 1 since they can exist in the position of these two states.

You can think of a qubit to a type of an imaginary sphere, which has two poles. For the case of a classical bit, it can only be in any of the two poles. For the case of a qubit, it can be at any particular point on the sphere. This is an indication that a computer that uses qubits can store much information by use of a less amount of energy compared to a classical computer.

Once functional quantum computers have been released, they will be able to read the secret messages that are communicated over the internet by use of the current technologies such as Diffie-Hellman, RSA and other cryptography problems.

With quantum computers, scientists will be able to use them to conduct virtual experiments. Quantum computing started after Feynman discovered that it is hard to model quantum systems on a conventional computer. If there was a quantum computer today, it would have been used in modelling quantum systems. This technique is referred to as *quantum simulation*. Example, we can model the behavior of particles and atoms at unusual conditions. We can also model chemical reactions since the interactions amongst the atoms in the chemical reaction are also a quantum process.

Quantum computers can be used to search huge amounts of data. Suppose you have a large phone book with a long list of people's names, and these have been ordered using letters of the alphabet. If you need the name of the individual with a particular phone number in the phone book, we must go through the list of all the names while checking their phone numbers and comparing it with the number we have.

If you have stored millions of phone numbers in the phone book, then it will also take a million steps for you to complete the task. If you have stored one million phone numbers, a quantum computer can do the task with only 1000 steps rather than 1 million steps. Quantum computers will be very useful anytime we need to find something in some large amount of data.

You may also have a large database of numbers and your goal is to find some numbers say two numbers. If you are having hundreds of thousands of numbers in the database, it will take a classical computer the same number of steps to find the two numbers. However, a quantum computer is capable of doing it within a shorter amount of time.

Such benefits of quantum computing are borrowed from quantum mechanics. They are known as *quantum interference* and *quantum parallelism*.

For a conventional computer to process data, it must encode it into bits, that is, 0s and 1s. If the computer has a sequence of thirty 0s and 1s, there will be one billion possible values. For the case of a classical computer, it is only capable of being in only one of these billion states at any particular time.

When it comes to a quantum computer, it is capable of being in a quantum combination of all of these states, and this is known as *superposition*. This means that the computer is capable of performing a billion computations or so at the same time. This can be compared to a parallel computer having one billion processors that are performing different tasks simultaneously. However, a difference exists between these two. For the case of the parallel computer, we should have one different billion processors. For the case of the quantum computer, all the one billion computations will be running on the same hardware. This is what is referred to as *quantum parallelism.*

The result of such a process is a quantum process encoding results of the one billion computations. However, the person who designs algorithms for a quantum computer will experience a challenge. How can these billion results be accessed? After measuring the quantum state, only one of the results will be obtained, and the rest of the results will disappear.

To solve the above problem, one should use the property of *quantum interference*. Suppose you have another problem capable of arriving at the same outcome via a number of different ways. Non-quantumly, with two paths leading to the same result in which every path has been taken with a probability of ¼; the overall probability for obtaining the result will be ¼ + ¼ = ½. When it comes to the quantum world, the two paths may interfere and the probability of success will be increased to 1.

Quantum algorithms are capable of combining these two effects. With quantum parallelism, one can perform a large number of computations at the same time. While quantum interference helps one combines the results in order to get something that is more meaningful and measurable using the quantum mechanics laws.

However, there is a challenge in building some large-scale quantum computer. There are a number of ways through which one can do this. The best results so far have been obtained by use of trapped ions. An ion is simply an atom that has lost one or more of its electrons. The ion trap is a system made up of electric and magnetic fields, capable of capturing ions and keeping them at locations. By use of an ion trap, one is able to arrange the ions in some line, even at regular intervals.

It is possible to encode 0 to lowest energy state of ion and 1 into higher energy state. The computation can then be done by use of light in order to manipulate the states of the ions.

In an experiment done at University of Innsbruck, Austria, this has successfully been done for up to 14 ions. In the next step, the technology will be scaled up to some bigger number of trapped ions.

There are several other ways to building a quantum computer. Rather than using the trapped ions, one can choose to use particles or electrons of light photons. It is possible to use complicated objects such as electric current in a superconductor. The good with all these physical systems such as atoms and the electric current in a semiconductor exhibit a behavior that is in line to same physical laws. They are all capable of performing quantum computation. However, it will be difficult for us to isolate the quantum systems from the environment and be able to operate them with a high level of precision. This is very hard and a fundamental task and it will be very useful for us to control quantum systems.

Quantum mechanics may be used for description of many physical systems and each system has its own technical details. Also, there are sets of principles that these physical systems should obey. The focus of quantum information is on principles that can be commonly applied to all the quantum systems. After reading quantum information well, you will be acquainted very well with the basics of quantum mechanics.

A technique known as quantum tunneling is believed to make quantum computers more energy efficient compared to classical computers. This is why quantum computers are expected to reduce power consumption by 100 to 1000 times. The Deep Blue computer of IBM is capable of processing 200 million moves in each second. A quantum computer will be able to calculate one trillion of such moves in a second. Quantum computers need cold temperatures for operation. They are also expected to speed up the speed of learning in artificial intelligence (AI) and thousands of learning years are expected to be reduced to seconds.

However, it is worth to note that quantum computers are not made to perform basic tasks such as sending of emails. They are designed to be used in solving complex tasks and the ones that conventional computers are unable to perform. Of course, there are such problems, even some algorithms. These will be done using quantum computers. This is why quantum computers are not expected to replace the classical computers completely.

Quantum computers will be able to hack into any private data stored on the internet. Normally, such data is encrypted using classical cryptography mean for security purposes.

However, the classical cryptography will not be jeopardized completely. Some of its features will be jeopardized, but quantum mechanics provides us with a way of securing data which is highly secure.

Consider a popular cryptographic protocol known as *one-time pad*. Suppose you have two parties, Alice and Bob. The two shares a long string made up of random 0s and 1s, and this forms the *secret key*. If they are the only ones who know the key and they use it for only once, they will be able to transmit a secret message and no eavesdropper will be able to decipher it. However, there is a problem with the one-time pad protocol, which is the distribution of the secret key. Quantum mechanics comes in to help us in this using a technique known as *Quantum Key Distribution (QKD)*. This technique allows for the distribution of random keys at a distance.

The quantum key distribution technique depends on a very interesting feature of quantum mechanics, which is that any attempt to measure or observe a quantum system disturbs it.

Chapter 4- Will they Replace Classical Computers?

Quantum computers have grabbed the attention of people throughout the world, and now they seem to be entering the commercial space. Quantum computers can be used to find the prime factors of a number, which can be used to break the security provided by the RSA algorithm, which is the most popular method of encryption in use today.

If the quantum computers are capable of factoring large numbers quickly, then the security of the internet will be rendered obsolete. Research is being done to establish the use of quantum computers in molecular modelling. To model even the simplest computers in the world with a classical computer, it may take years. Molecular modelling can be applied in development of effective medicines, finding the best catalysts, and even the manufacture of new drugs and other materials, and this can disrupt these industries. The Haber-Bosch which is a process for preparation of Ammonia and fertilizers is too energy intensive, hence it is an area of research.

Quantum computers can accelerate the development of machine learning systems which can be used in driverless cars, robotics, automation, pattern recognition etc.

These fields require computers with high processing capacity; hence quantum computers will be very applicable here. Quantum computers are capable of solving computation intensive optimization problems.

Quantum computers will be used in areas of scientific research such as calculation of reaction rates, modelling interior of Black holes, combustion as well as other effects.

However, despite the fact that quantum computers are capable of solving problems faster than classical computers, there are a number of problems that they can't solve. An example of such a problem is the NP complete problem which is very popular in computing. This problem is verifiable within a polynomial time but there is no way that is known to find a solution to the problem. Neither quantum nor classical computers can solve such problems within polynomial time.

In quantum computers, the qubits should remain entangled, that is, whatever happens to one should affect the other instantly, even in cases where they are in different locations. Classical computers do not rely on superposition and entanglement effects.

Transistors are getting smaller and classical computers should avoid quantum effect, as the quantum computers gainfully use them.

The major challenge in the development of quantum computers has been the development of qubits capable of satisfying the required conditions. Qubits normally lose superposition and this leads to decoherence in which the system becomes entangled with the environment. This happens very quickly, leaving on the classical states. If there are shorter coherent times, then the calculations will be prone to errors. However, it is possible to correct such errors by use of quantum error correction technique but long calculation times are needed. However, the challenge is on increasing decoherence time. The environment is the one that causes decoherence; hence we need to isolate the system from the environment.

Due to the above challenge, several methods for developing qubits have been developed. Google and IBM have successfully built their qubits from superconducting materials. Intel and some other companies are working with qubits that have been fabricated from tiny silicon bits called *quantum dots*. D-Wave makes use of niobium loops as qubits.

A small company known as *Quantum Circuits* is creating small machines then networking them together in a bid to reduce the error rates.

The qubits may be ions that have been trapped then manipulated by use of lasers or photons inside optical cavities. Most of these methods operate at methods that are near absolute zero as this helps in reducing decoherence time.

Quantum computers have beyond theoretical possibility space and they are now entering commercial space. However, quantum computers are expensive and bulky. This is because the use of common methods such as quantum annealing, superconducting circuits and others are in need of cryogenics in order to function. There are also energy implications when it comes to maintain such low temperatures. This is why they have large cylindrical freezers, wires and other components. The process is just a small part of it. Secondly, quantum computers will excel in problems that are perceived to be difficult for classical computers. The quantum computers will still be relying on classical sequencing as well as classical control on the operations. There are numerous areas in which quantum algorithms capable of showing improvement over the classical areas do not exist.

The experience of the end user for average user won't change. In the next decade, quantum computers will be used commercially. However, classical computers will still be used as computing machines. This means that quantum computers will be put into practice, but they will not replace the classical computers. Quantum computers will help in solving complex problems that classical computers have not been able to solve. They will also help in solving problems that take classical computers a long amount of time to solve faster. However, quantum computers will be inappropriate for solving normal tasks that are normally solved efficiently using the classical computers.

A quantum computer will be able to find the best material for a particular task, quantum computers will be able to search through millions of materials and choose the best one. A good application of this is when finding ultra strong polymers to be used in making airplane wings. Advertisers can use quantum algorithms to improve the recommendations for their products. Scientists will make use of quantum computers in exploring the exotic realms of physics and in simulation of what may happen deep in a black hole. Quantum computers will also boost the efforts of individuals who doing research about machine learning.

They will lead to a near flawless recognition of handwriting and help driverless cars in assessing the flood of data pouring from sensors to be able to avoid hitting a child who is getting into the street.

However, for quantum computers to be able to reach their full potential, the power of millions of qubits will need to be harnessed, and this may take more than a decade.

The goal of classical computing is to perform numerous computations within the shortest period of time possible, and these computations are complete in a fair number of steps. This is not what happens in algorithms such as the brute-force cracking algorithms in which a large number of possible outcomes are taken and the computer scans through each of them in a step-by-step manner. This creates locks in areas such as encryption, but such level of fuzzy logic is not applicable in simple operations where it is beneficial to perform calculations in series rather than in parallel.

The best way to do computations is in series and rapidly since algorithms work in a similar way. Development of quantum algorithms takes a lot of new thinking. Suppose you need to take a trip round woods. You can choose to scan the area, or just take a walk on the ground.

The latter is more effective compared to the former. Quantum computers will not be much useful like the classical computers. They will only be applied in a number of tasks, especially the ones that are require more computing resources. This means that individuals who only use computers for basic tasks may not need to use the quantum computers. This is why quantum computers will not completely replace the classical computers.

Most people use computers to perform only basic tasks. These including typing, browsing the internet, playing music etc. classical computers have proved to be excellent in these tasks. Most companies also rely on computers for the basic tasks. Quantum computers will only be used by companies that require computers with high computing power in terms of processing speed. In fact, quantum computers will be well applicable in server environments as server computers should have a high processing power.

Chapter 5- Areas to be Revolutionized by Quantum Computers

Quantum computing has attracted a high attention. A lot of money is now being poured into research about quantum computers with people in both the private and public sector believing that quantum computers are the next big thing in computing. So far, it has been proved that quantum computers will be able tom solve some computational tasks within a shorter period of time compared to classical computers. Due to this, quantum computers could be highly applicable in numerous science and business areas.

There is a great reason as to why big IT companies in the world such as Google, IBM and Microsoft are heavily investing in quantum computing. Of course, you cannot invest where you don't see any potential. These companies have seen that quantum computers will change the world by solving the problems that classical computers have not been able to.

Quantum computers are expected to bring a disruption to every industry in the world. They will change the way business is done, the way we secure data on the internet as well as offline, how diseases are prevented and new materials discovered and how heath and climatic problems are solved.

The race towards creating the first quantum computer is accelerating, and below are some of the industries that will be affected or changed by quantum computing:

1. Online security
   Quantum computers will be good and bad for online security. The bad thing is that they will make the online security techniques used currently obsolete. Majority of security mechanisms used to secure online data rely on the fact that it takes a classical computer or a human individual a long period of time to crunch large set of numbers. However, when it comes to quantum computers, this can be done within a short amount of time. This means that our private data and financial institutions will be left vulnerable. However, to counter this, a lot has been done towards coming up with quantum encryption methods like quantum key distribution. In this method, a key will be required in order to decipher a message.

2. Artificial Intelligence
   Quantum computers are suitable for processing information that can bring a lot of change to the machine learning world. Machine learning relies on huge amounts of data from which patterns and trends are extracted. Companies are also

generating a lot of data each day, meaning that a lot of data will be available in the next few years. Classical computers are finding it hard to extract patterns and trends from big data. However, quantum computers will be able to extract patterns and trends from huge data repositories in within a short period of time. This means that quantum computers will shorten the learning curve for quantum computers. With quantum computers, artificial intelligence will expand hugely and it will be applied to many industries. In artificial intelligence, systems need to search from video, audio and image contents. This has been a hard task for the classical computers. This is due to the fact that such files are heavy and they need computers with high processing capabilities. Quantum computers are going to change this completely. It will be possible to track stolen cars using images of quantum computers and even lost individuals. Of course, a task such as tracking a lost individual via gadgets such as CCTVs will involve processing a large number of images of persons, maybe persons passing along a particular street. Such task can only be achieved using a computer with high processing capability. A quantum computer will be able to process such images in the shortest time possible and identify the individual if spotted. Currently, this is impossible with the classical computers.

3. Drug development
   To develop an effective drug, there is a need to evaluate the interactions between molecules, chemicals and proteins in order and determine whether the resulting medicine will be able to cure diseases or improve certain conditions. A high number of combinations will have to be evaluated, making this process intensive in terms of labor and time. Due to the ability of quantum computers to analyze multiple molecules, chemicals and proteins at the same time, they provide chemists with a better and effective way of finding effective drugs quickly. Quantum computers will also make the process of personal drug development much easy. They will provide a way to sequence and analyze personal genes more rapidly when compared to the methods that are used today. The components of various molecules as well as their interactions with other molecules will be analyzed with much ease, and insights which could not be gained using a classical computer will be gained. Some diseases are not curable today. With quantum computers, interactions between complex molecules to unearth even the finest details in this, and this may lead to the

discovery of new drugs that can help in curing some of the diseases that are not curable today. A good example of such a disease is HIV/AIDS. This may lead to saving of lives and long life expectancy.

4. Traffic control
Quantum computers will help in streamlining traffic control, both on the ground and in the air. Using quantum computers, we will be able to reduce traffic congestion by quickly determining the optimal routes concurrently which will lead to efficient scheduling. Due to this ability of quantum computers, they can be used in supply chains, fleet operations, air traffic control and deliveries. The effect of this will be saving time as motorists will not waste much time in traffic jams. Quantum computers will provide a way of assessing various routes to know the best route to use, which should be the route with the least or no traffic congestion. This is good to the economies of the world as time wasted in traffic jams will be spend in production.

5. Weather forecasting
Even with the user of advanced tools, weather forecasting today remains a guess work. It has happened severally that people have been

caught in a storm when they were not expecting it. This has cost lives through accidents, especially air accidents. Quantum computers are capable of analyzing the data at once, and meteorologists will be able to know when storms will occur and this will help in saving time, money and even lives. Some of the companies that deal with weather forecasting have invested heavily bin quantum computing because they have seen the potential of it changing the weather forecasting sector. With quantum computers, it will be possible to build better climatic models, making it easy to know how the climate is being influenced. It will be easy to know or predict how things are going to change, hence take adequate preparations for climate change and its impacts.

6. Financial sector
   Financial institutions such as banks are generating a lot of financial data on a daily basis. This data remains un-analyzed up to date due to lack of adequate computing power to do so. Banks have made losses due to making of poor financial decisions. With a proper analysis of this data, banks and other financial institutions can gain insights from the data and use these in decision making. When using quantum computers, this is possible. Such

institutions can find new ways of modelling the financial data for their own benefit. It then becomes easy to identify some of the risky areas and undertakings and if avoided, the institution will avoid making losses. These can also help the institution in making better and sound decisions. They can also take advantage of such insights to make better investment decisions.

7. Supply Chain & Logistics

   Quantum computers will help in finding best solutions for global supply chains and ultra-efficient logistics like optimizing the fleet operations for delivery of goods and services during the holiday season. A good example is an airline logistics manager who needs to offer the best airline services at a lower cost. Or a factory manager for a factory whose machines, production orders, inventory and people keep on changing and there is a need to minimize costs while maximizing the output. Classical computers have been used to solve such problems, but some of such tasks may be complicated to be done using a classical computer. A quantum computer can do it better. In classical computers, troubleshooting issues is done bit after a bit.

With quantum computers, the entire problem is tackled at once. This way, amazing avenues are opened up for each and every field that you know, including financial and national security.

Quantum computers may improve cyber security. With the increase in the number of available hacking tools, most of which are provided for free, there is a need to come up with ways to secure government and organization data. The current data security tools can be breached by use of these tools, and sometime, with much ease. Quantum computers will provide new, powerful and more secure ways of encrypting data. It is possible to ensure that the data can only be decrypted or hacked by an individual using a quantum computer. Since quantum computers will be scarce, it may mean that it will be hard to hack into that, improving the security of the data.

When functional quantum computers are finally developed, technology geeks will have to use the quantum encryption methods in order to secure both online and offline data. Failure to do so will lead to data security breaches. However, the quantum computers may be too expensive for one to afford. This means that individuals may need to hack using a quantum computer, but they can't afford to get one, which is a major advantage.

Also, quantum computers may be used only by bigger companies that need a high amount of processing power. The issue of cost is also significant. Not all companies will be able to afford to purchase quantum computers. This means that classical computers will still be widely used even after the development of a functional quantum computer. If quantum encryption methods are used to encrypt both online and offline data, it means that there will be an improved data security. A classical computer can never hack data that has been encrypted using quantum encryption methods. For it to do so, it may take a long period of time even years. This means that hacking using classical computers will be highly reduced.

So far, the quantum data encryption and key distribution methods have shown that classical computers cannot overcome. A lot is still being discovered about quantum computing and new discoveries about how to secure data may be discovered. Although quantum computers will bring issues to do with data security, they will make it hard for individuals using classical computers to hack into organization and company data.

Conclusion

This marks the end of this book. No functional quantum computer has been developed so far, but a lot of work has been done towards developing practical quantum computer. When developed, they will be able to perform tasks faster compared to the current classical computers. Quantum computers will be able to perform tasks that have proved to be complex for classical computers to perform. They are expected to change a lot of industries including weather forecasting, drug development, climatic change prediction, artificial intelligence etc. Although quantum computers will perform the tasks that classical computers have not been able to, they will not replace the classical computers. They will only be used for performing complex computations in which a high processing power is needed. For instance, quantum computers will be capable of searching a particular piece of data huge data repositories within seconds, a process that can take classical computer even hours. Currently, no functional quantum computer has been developed but a lot is being done to ensure that one enters the commercial space sooner.

Printed in Great Britain
by Amazon